FANtastic Franchises
HARRY POTTER FRANCHISE

Kenny Abdo

Fly!
An Imprint of Abdo Zoom
abdobooks.com

abdobooks.com

Published by Abdo Zoom, a division of ABDO, P.O. Box 398166, Minneapolis, Minnesota 55439. Copyright © 2025 by Abdo Consulting Group, Inc. International copyrights reserved in all countries. No part of this book may be reproduced in any form without written permission from the publisher. Fly!™ is a trademark and logo of Abdo Zoom.

Printed in the United States of America, North Mankato, Minnesota.
052024
092024

Photo Credits: Alamy, Everett Collection, Getty Images, Newscom, Shutterstock
Production Contributors: Kenny Abdo, Jennie Forsberg, Grace Hansen
Design Contributors: Candice Keimig, Neil Klinepier, Colleen McLaren

Library of Congress Control Number: 2023948522

Publisher's Cataloging-in-Publication Data

Names: Abdo, Kenny, author.
Title: Harry Potter franchise / by Kenny Abdo
Description: Minneapolis, Minnesota : Abdo Zoom, 2025 | Series: FANtastic franchises | Includes online resources and index.
Identifiers: ISBN 9781098285579 (lib. bdg.) | ISBN 9781098286279 (ebook) | ISBN 9781098286620 (Read-to-me eBook)
Subjects: LCSH: Warner Bros. Family Entertainment (Firm)--Juvenile literature. | Potter, Harry (Fictitious character)--Juvenile literature. | Rowling, J. K. Harry Potter series--Juvenile literature. | Wizards—Juvenile literature. | Branding (Marketing)--Juvenile literature. | Popular culture--Juvenile literature.
Classification: DDC 338.768--dc23

TABLE OF CONTENTS

Harry Potter 4

Origins 6

Through the Years.............. 10

Fandom 20

Glossary 22

Online Resources 23

Index 24

HARRY POTTER

From the halls of Hogwarts to Diagon Alley, Harry Potter is the most magical **franchise** in the world!

ORIGINS

Inspiration struck author J.K. Rowling in 1990 while on a delayed train traveling to London. The thought of a young boy who did not know he was a wizard popped into her head.

Unable to shake the idea, Rowling began work on a novel. She completed it in 1995. Most **publishers** rejected the book. Finally, Bloomsbury Publishing took a chance on the tale of Harry Potter.

THROUGH THE YEARS

Harry Potter and the Philosopher's Stone was released in the United Kingdom in 1997. It was an immediate hit! It was released in the United States one year later to even greater fanfare!

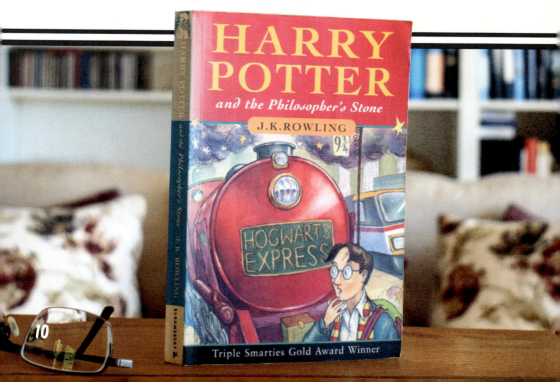

Six books followed almost yearly after. From *Harry Potter and the Chamber of Secrets* to *Harry Potter and the Deathly Hallows*, Rowling continued to expand the magical universe!

In 2001, the Harry Potter world came to life on the big screen! Unknown actor Daniel Radcliffe put on Harry's wizard robe for the role. It was the highest-**grossing** film of the year! Seven more films followed.

Each movie was loved by fans and critics. The films earned 12 **Academy Award** nominations. The series earned more than $7 billion!

In 2010, the Wizarding World of Harry Potter opened at Universal Islands of Adventure in Florida. Fans could also roam Diagon Alley when a second one opened at Universal Studios in 2014.

The themed lands include rides, shops, and dining straight from the series. They also feature a full recreation of Hogwarts castle! Lands opened in Japan, California, and China too.

The film *Fantastic Beasts and Where to Find Them* was released in 2016. It was **inspired** by the guide book Rowling wrote in 2001. The film featured exciting new characters and creatures from the Harry Potter universe.

Harry Potter and the Cursed Child opened in 2016. Based on a story by Rowling, the play takes place 19 years after the events of the last novel.

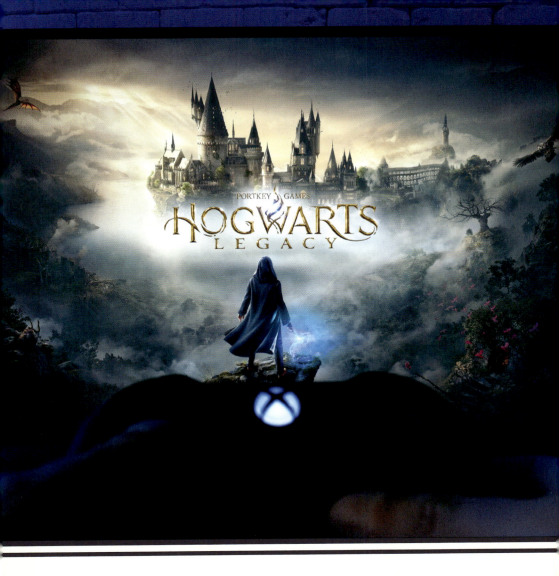

Dozens of video games have allowed fans to wield wands through the years. *Hogwarts Legacy* was released in 2023. It was one of the most successful games of the year with fans and in sales!

FANDOM

Throughout the years, fans have held many **conventions** celebrating the boy wizard. They have also created lots of **fanfiction**, including films, musicals, and plays.

The *Harry Potter* books have sold more than 500 million copies. They have been translated into 80 languages and made into eight **blockbuster** films. It's a feat almost as impressive as catching the Golden Snitch!

GLOSSARY

Academy Award – one of several awards the Academy of Motion Picture Arts and Sciences gives annually to achievement in the movie industry.

blockbuster – a movie that is incredibly popular and makes a lot of money.

convention – a gathering where fans of a franchise or topic come together to participate in events and meet experts, celebrities, and each other.

fanfiction – stories involving popular fictional characters from a certain TV series, movie, or other media that is written by fans.

franchise – a collection of related movies, TV shows, and other media in a series.

grossing – earning.

inspiration – to gain motivation or creativity from another source.

publisher – a company that oversees the editing, printing, and the selling of books.

ONLINE RESOURCES

To learn more about the Harry Potter franchise, please visit **abdobooklinks.com** or scan this QR code. These links are routinely monitored and updated to provide the most current information available.

INDEX

Academy Awards 14

fans 20

Fantastic Beasts and Where to Find Them (movie; book) 17

Harry Potter and the Chamber of Secrets (book) 11

Harry Potter and the Cursed Child (play) 18

Harry Potter and the Deathly Hallows (book) 11

Harry Potter and the Philosopher's Stone (book) 9, 10

Hogwarts Legacy (game) 19

movies 12, 14, 17, 21

Radcliffe, Daniel 12

Rowling, J.K. 6, 9, 11, 17, 18

Wizarding World of Harry Potter, The 15, 16